My Country Australia

by

I0173286

Elizabeth Waterhouse

© 2015 Shadowlight Publishing
Brisbane, Queensland, Australia

Dedication

I was blessed to be born in this beautiful country, surrounded by a loving family and encouraging wonderful friends. Every day is an exciting adventure. I thank Sue Manger for her friendship and proofreading of this book and also the genius writer and poet R.e.Taylor, and my best friend Robert Taylor for all his constant encouragement and support. I live on a island continent, but no man should be an island and to share one's dreams with such a brilliant man is everything and to have been able to show him as a visitor the beauty of Australia is such a joy. I love my country Australia and especially its warm and generous people!

Index

Australia

Australia

I was just a tourist
In a sun -kissed land
Now I'm a captive
To serve at her command

The Colours of Australia

The colours of Australia
Bright yellow and green
The haunting arid outback
And scenic pastoral scene
Soft white virgin sand
Coral reefs and inlet bays
Silvery moonlit nights
And red hot summer days
Lavender, vivid pink wild flowers
Brown earth and dusty plain
Aqua oceans, sparkling waters
Stark red ochre terrain
Orange crimson sunsets
Rainbows and skies of blue
Our emerald rainforests
Golden sunlight shining through
The colours of Australia
It's the gift we give to you.

God Bless The Tourists

Bloody strewth mate look out here they come
The Tourists Down-Under to have some fun
Clickin' their cameras, lookin' goggle- eyed
While out in the hot sun getting deep fried
Askin' for service and getting in our hair
Makes you wonder if they're really all there
Thinkin' it's Spring in the middle of May
Speakin' a foreign lingo, as they say G'Day

Forget we're multi-cultural and highly urbanized
Give 'em the Aussie salute that the ads advertise
Imports are out, the Aussie image wins
Now here's where yer work it really begins
Wear Moleskins, an Akubra, Drizabone
Hide the credit cards and Bluetooth phone
Cover the microwave, throw out Sarah Lee
From now on its damper, pavlova and billy tea

Yack about the outback and the old pioneers
Have a bush barbie, and down a few beers
Quote a couple of verses from old Banjo
Hobnob round the fire, put on a dinkum show
Get out the four wheel and take 'em for a drive
Never mention our crocs can eat you alive
Ignore all snakes, sharks, mozzies and the flies
Crows flying backwards, and them peckin' magpies

Explain that kangaroos don't hop down our streets
Nor for breakfast do we bush tucker eats
Throw a boomerang, take me to a Corroboree
Tell 'em the tour guides take care of the fee
Bush dances are popular, and so is Uluru
Dingoes, frilled lizards and wallaby stew
Show em the Australia that we've never seen
Mate, tourists on nature are so bloody keen

Let 'em hug a koala, they're as cute as can be
Just watch the bloody bastards don't on 'em pee
Before they go home, help them spend all their loot
Then add departure tax, so they're real destitute.
Sing "Waltzing Matilda", "Advance Australia Fair"
In those tourist dollars, we all want to share
This Aussie image to some may seem passé
Mate, you watch 'em flock here, so remember G'Day!

Virgin Sand

Come with me to my hideaway
Enchanted land so far away
Lapping waves and summer breeze
Moonlight glistening through the trees

Come with me to my tropic land
Walk with me on my virgin sand
My love for you was never planned
My virgin, virgin, pure white sand

Though I travel far and wide
To distant lands so glorified
My thoughts always return to thee
My tropic isle across the sea

Come with me to a land so grand
Tropic Island clear white sand
The paradise where I'll make my bed
Caressed by the Southern Cross overhead

Come with me to deep waters blue
Shangri-la for you and me
Come with me to a wonderland
My virgin land of pure white sand.

The Rain

Red sand dunes, cane grass, dry mallee
Blazing sun, creating a mirage like sea
Thirsting bush, dry, dusty plain
As the rain once more brings life again.

On Eagles Wings

Come fly with me on eagles wings
Forgetting time and evolution
And I will show you wonderous things
Not marred by man's pollution.

The States Of Australia

New South Wales

Infant child of Penal birth
Golden sands and white capped peaks
Glistening towers, in the sky
Lakes, billabongs and creeks
Bureaucrats, convict and free settler
They survived and even thrived
Then Overlander, Shearer and Drover
For a better life they strived
The memories of gold fever
And Federation soon begun
This great land is a testimony
To the Victory they had won
River gums on the Murray
Our capital territory and parliament house
Sydney's beautiful Harbour
And our famous Opera House
Wattle and flaming Waratah
Country pubs and old homesteads
Sailing boats on Sydney Harbour
Grazing land and tin woolsheds
Rainforests, Alpine chalets
Wilderness, and super highways
Farms, bushland, woods, picturesque beaches

Starry nights and sun swept days
Land of the endeavor, forever calling me
Land begun in bondage, of convict pedigree
Land of our beginnings in old Botany
Essence of Australia, first Penal Colony.

Tasmania

The enticing grandeur of our Island State
National parks and lofty mountains
Highland lakes and historic towns
Cascading waterfalls, orchards, lavender fields
Alluring, majestic Island of one's dreams
Remote beaches, and glistening white sand
Rainforests, rivers and rippling streams
Old fishing villages, coves and inlet bays
Sun of molten gold, skies of misty blue
Tall trading ships, the twilight's silvery glow
An unexplored wilderness beckons to you
Peaceful rainbow land, of infinite beauty
Where the past and the present interlace
People and nature in perfect harmony
A magical island, where we our dreams embrace.

South Australia

Take me home where the eagles fly
To the land of sun and cloudless sky
Flinders Ranges, Peninsulas and Plains
Wilderness, red ochre surreal terrain
Hairy Nosed Wombat, Sturt's Desert Pea
Picture postcard villages and rolling hills
The Barossa Valley our winemakers' skills
Blue waters of the Great Australian Bight
Sunlit skies and starry rhapsodic nights
The Simpson Desert and its red sand dunes
As wild flowers this sunburnt land festoons
Kangaroo Island, vast cattle properties
Proclamation Day and the old Gum Tree
Woomera, Blue Lagoon, Adelaide, and salt lakes
Land of flaming skies, all our emotion awakes.

Victoria

Behold the scenic splendour
Of our glorious Garden State
Alps, valleys and rich pastures
A colourful canvas create
Dairy, sheep, wool and cattle
Bountiful catches from the sea
Citrus farms and wineries
Vast riches all can see
The Diggers and The Gold Rush
Gold nuggets mud and clay.
Clunes, Ballarat and Bendigo
And the Eureka stockade
Where the flag of the Southern Cross
In rebellion there was raised
The legendary Ned Kelly
Our rebels so often praised
The floodlit plains of the Murray
Irrigation our dry lands change
Lakes, dams, the Shipwreck Coast
The Great Dividing Range
Melbourne, our stately capital
With its gardens, parks and trees
Commerce, Sports, Arts and Culture
A metropolis the aesthetics, please

Wild flowers dance across the land
Autumn leaves and summer flowers
Land of charismatic charm
Breathtaking, serene beauty, so gracious and grand.

Queensland

Rainforests and sparkling white sand
Brisbane and friendly country towns
Man eating crocodiles
Outback and Darling Downs
Sun- kissed colours like a rainbow
Blue skies, wattle and waratah
The Daintree, grey dingo fence
The pink and white galah
The awe inspiring Barrier Reef
Tropical beaches, reefs and isles
Swaying palms and humpback whales
"Tropic Madness" on everyone smiles
Sailors, miners, drovers and tourists
Developers with their saws
Sharks, typhoons, toads and rabbits
They all come to our shores
Rich brown earth and floodlit plain
Burnt scrub and sugar cane
The tropic shower, the hurricane
The constant cry for rain
Lazy days and shimmering haze
And starry moonlit nights
Thirsting bush and blinding dust
The heat the earth ignites

People, animals and solitude
Earth's bounty here we sow
Gum trees, beaches and billabongs
Paradise untamed aglow.

Western Australia

Land of shipwrecks and sailors
From far and distant lands
Where scorched earth greets the day
And the giant boab stands
Land of the Dreamtime
Of a million starry nights
Of Aboriginal corroborees
And sacred tribal rights
Sea swept, sun- kissed
Where galahs and eagles soar
Spinifex and wild flowers
Covering the lands rich core
Land of the "Willy Willy"
Perth and Nullarbor Plain
Kimberley, Ord River,
Last cattle King's domain
Land of coal and diamonds
And pearls in oyster bed
Of conquest and hardship
The survivors here are bred
Kaleidoscope of colour
Earth's bounty royally dressed
Such awe inspiring beauty
With God's riches we are blessed.

Northern Territory

Stark barren red island
Rising out of sea like sand
Changing colours reflecting
The heat and sun parched land
The shadows cast by the Olgas
Beneath a rainbow sky
Land eternal revolving
Interchanging wet and dry
Like a speck of sand in time
Are the prints of all of man
Ancient land of cycads
The hot, dry breezes fan
A pitiless barren country
Giving birth to evergreen
Ghost gums like sentinels
On solitary escarpments wean
Kakadu and Katherine
And the emblem Kangaroo
Solitude, the Dreamtime
And the sacred Uluru
Heart of this my country
Pulsating barren land
Land of "The Never Never"
This Northern wonderland.

True Blue
Real Dinkum
Aussie Verse

The Great Aussie Picnic

The mozzies are biting, we forgot the Aeroguard
The ants, all the bikkies are about to bombard
The twins are fightin' and actin' real mean
This family picnic, it's a real bloody scene
The baby's cryin' 'cause he bashed both 'is knees
The flies in the marg, and the dogs got the cheese
Gran's gone walkabout lookin' for the lav
Cripes, there's a Kookaburra, poopin' on the Pav!
Young Curly's so famished, he's eatin' mud pies
And Bluey's being chased by some peckin' magpies
Dave's bashin' his missus and actin' like a lout
She forgot the plonk and the beers run out
Old gramps at the barbie burnin' the snags
Dad's really cussin' 'cause Mum's snitched his fags
Now the tuckers ready as the rain in buckets pours
Strewth! Another get together in the great outdoors!

The Melbourne Cup

Like frilled lizards
In nature's finery dressed
The ladies of the Melbourne Cup
With hats are obsessed.

The Great Wonders Down-Under

Kookaburra laughing in the old gum tree
As the old swaggie brews his Billy tea
Come on Down-Under there's lots to see
Sunshine and freedom a real symphony
Of animals and nature in real harmony
See Aboriginals dance a corroboree
Outback, rainforests, scrub and mallee
The Barrier Reef and our bountiful sea
There's tucker, stubbies, birds and barbies
Our cities, beaches and Aussie Rules footie
Uluru, Kakadu, dingoes and wild brumbies
Kangaroos, koalas, and the Sydney Oprey
Mate, it's bonza Down-Under you'll all agree
With real beaut fair dinkum hospitality.

Condolences To James

No longer are we isolated,
In this far away country,
With the toys of modern society,
Internet and satellite TV.
A little picture tube,
That brings the world to our shore;
The Universe is at our doorstep,
Knocking at our door;
Bringing crisis and drama,
That we heedlessly consume

Tonight it's World Recession
Right in our living room;
Isn't it amazing!
T'would give Captain Cook a shock
New Holland sure has changed James
Now don't go off your block
Britannia doesn't rule supreme,
Her powers not worth a cent
The Colony's now a Nation,
With its own Government:

Terrorists, skyscrapers and ATM's
Drugs, You Tube, iPads modern machines
Don't worry Royalty's intact
The Queens not into jeans
Stop fuming in your grave James!
No need to shout and cuss!
There's talk of a Republic,
So you'll soon be rid of us!
And there's Charles and Camilla
So I won't dig in the knife

Crickey you're going down the gurgler
Strewth you're in a lot of strife.
Mate, we're now the clever country
Even in cricket you failed the Test
You're even part of the Common Market
Now James don't get so distressed
Yes life has changed since Botany Bay
Now James do not work up a sweat
Today we're all in glorious unison
As we chat on the Internet

You'd be surprised who you meet on the street
Terrorism is now just everywhere
Even soccer now reigns supreme
Now James, stop tearing out your hair
Sorry,"Rule Britannia"it sure is out of date
America now maintains the dominant place
You no longer rule the waves
Fair dinkum, we're also proud to show our face
As today, we've come of age
Your Aussie convict slaves.

Troppo Up North

Come on mate let's sally forth
Let's go troppo way up North
Swaying palms and balmy breezes
Who wants to be where you bloody freezes

So shed those woolies catch a plane
Come on mate-let's live again
Slap on a hat so you don't get sunstroke
Come up North and have some fun folk

Down by the pool let the good times rip
Let's go troppo so start to strip
Bird watching here is highly recommended
Frolicking in the sun as nature intended

Now careful those necks you don't dislocate
As on our native fauna you concentrate
Birds and sheilas we've got galore
Sun bronzed blokes woman can't ignore

Forget the Reef and Hump Back Whales
Bungee jumping and old winding trails
Bush walking really works up a sweat
And Rainforests only get you wet

Much better mate to stay at the pool
Recharge those batteries, time to refuel
Our swanky resorts are really first rate
Mate, grab a beer and luxuriate

Don't mind the mozzies or Dengue fever
Swipe the flies as you wave at a sheila
Going troppo mate, you'll be busy as can be
Lazing in the sun by a shady palm tree.

Aussie Product Scene

We Aussie like to have a bite
Of bread and butter and vegemite
We'll save a Crumble bar for you
Cherry Ripe and Lamingtons too
With snags and meat pies all life long
Instant Pavlovas just seems all wrong
Aussie owned Coopers brings real cheer
While in Britian they brew our Fosters beer
Now Gran, took Vincents with confidence
Bushels tea is Mum's preference
She takes the tea with Sarah Lee
Guess they're both not quite Aussie
Neither is Arnotts, or Lean Cuisine
Times have changed in the tucker scene
Eating at the pics with my mates
Minties and Jaffa chocolates
Now the swaggie my mates and me
We really like strong Billy tea
Damper and meat pies still true blue
Aussie products for me and you
But on take out we're now real keen
Steak, fish and chips hardly ever seen
Maccas seems to be the choice of the day

Give me our dinky die barbies, is all I can say
Even the bloody Kiwis are claiming our Pav
Enough to send one heading for the lav
One has to adjust, with No Fosters in any pub
It's coke and meatballs, at the nearest Sub
Cripes! For kangaroo meat the prices now are high
Still, crocodile's dinkum tucker I cannot deny.
Even though the Yanks grab all that they can
Mate,, witchety grubs just ain't in their plan!

The Sanctimonious Pacifist

One considers oneself a non-violent type of person
I even give dead birds, and frogs a funeral with flowers
But in my kitchen, suddenly all hell breaks loose
When all is blackness and nothing but a sea of ants
Suddenly I go berserk, the killer instinct comes into play
Madness rips through me as I grab a spray gun in hand
The ants are defenceless, for them, it's an atomic bomb
I destroy sisters, brothers, even babies, just any ant in sight
Kill, Kill, Kill, destroy, destroy, destroy, spray, spray, spray
The masses, trillions, that invade my white kitchen floor
All are swept into oblivion, offering no mercy,
Just their enemy with a spray gun pure hate and rage
Hate welling up inside me, the humanitarian gone mad
Screaming, die, die, die! as I wipe my enemy away
Then white floor gleaming, and everything back to norm
But then I ask myself, haven't I just killed a living thing
Lady,be aware you with views of non- violence in this world
You too are capable of hate and evil, just ask that helpless little
ant.

Wombats, Koalas and Kangaroos

Wombats, Koalas and Kangaroos
Down in Sydney's Taronga Park Zoo
Frilled lizards, Wallabies and Emu
Tasmanian Tiger, Goanna and Echidna too
G'Day mate! G'day mate! Says the Cockatoo
Making one hell of a halloo balloo
The kookaburra laughs till he nearly turns blue
As the Duck Bill Platypus comes into view
At tucker the Wombat chats with the old Gnu
"Pity you and the Kiwis ain't Aussie too!"
"So what about the Camels, Rabbits and Jabiru? "
"Oh no they're Aussie! Like shrimps on the barbeque!"
Says the sarcastic Prawn to the retinue
The Dingo slinks off for a late rendezvous
With the Crocodile who's a real yahoo
Mate, watch out they don't make a meal of you
Down in Sydney's Taronga Park Zoo
Wombats, Koalas and Kangaroo.

A Tribute To Bird Watchers

Now bird watchers are a plenty in this Aussie land
Appreciating in awe such beauty, flying or not
Admiring a tail whether coloured or curvy
Sweet chicks, colourful lorikeets, lovebirds, turtle doves
Birds that are scavengers, and some that devour their prey
Crazy cuckoos, or birds of paradise so well plumed
Now that sends bird watchers appreciation really soaring
Streuth, our birds with big breasts are really appealing
Yet skinny or big, they admire them all
To bag tasty tucker, that's the bird hunters dream
Now our Aussie birds they come in all shapes and sizes
A bird watchers delight gazed at and admired in awe
Yes, bird lovers, one can surely find a choice of birds here
So go for it mate, appreciate Aussie nature and all it entails
WARNING! Some Aussie birds peck when grabbing their tail!

Sombre Reflections

The Land

Parched earth and atrophied gums
Visible through clouds of dust
Flies round dead cattle hum
Ashes to ashes, dust to dust
As man to the land succumbs.

Complacency

Please save Australia"
The young Greenie cries
"In your complacency
Its destruction lies!"

The Tree

The tree that proudly in the forest stands
Providing shelter and sustaining life
Is being destroyed by the victims
Of a world heading to its own destruction.

Bludgers All

The rain this land in chaos throws
As rivers fill and overflow
Where is the day not long ago
We dreamed and the seeds did sow
Now mud and stench and drowning stock
As to the bank, we battlers flock
Bloody hell, we're a surviving breed
We cockies, I'll plant again our seeds
And when all else fails
We'll hang on by our fingernails
"Don't worry, she'll be right mate
Good times around the corner wait!"
Then droughts and floods, our dreams impede
As with foreclosure the banks proceed
"Bloody hell! Through dust and mud, we strived
Now with Government handouts are supplied
Flaming' bludgers, swept in by the tide
While the blood suckers take our land to subdivide
As in the receivers' hands, all our dreams they die
"Lucky Country", what a bloody lie!

The Cockies Lament

The Cockies are in trouble
They can't live off the land
Mortgaged out of existence
With their need to expand
Hope like the land eroded
Their luck just running out
Bushies always fighting
Fire, floods and drought
The Banks the terror every cockie dreads
As they climb into debt
To pay the overdraft
In the cities do we really care
About their rural problems
The despair the Bushies share
We know these rich farmers
Live off the fat of the land
Must be crazy thinking sugar
A great way to expand
Naive farmers watching crops
Rise in world market shares
Then dropping to the bottom
With prices they can't meet
A fair go to the farmers
The new cry in the street
Payment upon payment
More borrowing to survive
Friendly creditors turn nasty
Destroying many lives

Some still try to keep their head above water
As now shattered lie their dreams
Australia, where are you heading
Disillusioned cockies scream
While Bankers held in high esteem
Demand the money, all paid back
And so the mortgage holders
Reap the rural lands outback
Farms, cattle and sheep stations
For generations all family owned
By proud settlers and farmers
Now the kings are soon dethroned
By outsiders, prices and rising taxes
The creditors, Government and Banks
The bottom of the barrel
The farmers only thanks
Many facing foreclosure
They have no where else to go
While others are trying desperately
Some new profitable seed to sow
Farms soon under the hammer
To the foreign bidders sold.

Black Velvet

Pretty black velvet
Don't stay with him tonight
Rape and deprivation
Not your only birthright.

Indigenous Lament

They conquered my land
They stole it away
Made a ball of my head in the sand
So black fella, dies
As white fella, lies
For assimilation we qualifies
They took away our babies
Make a good life for 'em
No ifs, or buts, or maybes
With drink and the Mission
They broke up tradition
For marriage, white fella permission
Black fellas in shanties now congregate
Even though for thousand of years
We this place did habitate
White fella does what he will
With trees and land fill
As our land he continues to kill.

A Warning

Acid rain,climate change,toxic oil spill
Pollution, dying forests, plastic landfill
A dying species, chemical warfare, abortion the pill
With complacency and greed this earth we kill
Manipulated people, lost all hopes and dreams
The masses subjugated, nothing what it seems
Disillusioned children, rebellion in a gang
Fragmented parents trying to understand
Crime and violent anger, anarchy is what they breed
Abuse and intolerance, how well we sow the seed
Senseless violence that no one wants or needs
Communication constantly on negativity it feeds
Drugs and self absorption, youth that only take
Shattered obligations, such shit of life we make.

Naked Babe Of Innocence

Naked babe of innocence, in floppy blue sun hat
Sitting on a deck chair, like some ancient autocrat
Rosy cheeks, sparkling eyes, a child with enchanting grin
Covered in creams and lotions, to protect his tender skin.
A little girl approaches, cajoling him to play,
She gently tugs his arm, and entices him away

Running to the water, she squeals with pure delight,
He offers her his bucket, as two little souls unite.
Together building castles, in the virgin golden sand
Two little children together, lost in their wonderland.
Another season just begun, on this carefree summer's day
The beach is filled with people, just glad to get away.

Men away from worries, in the sunshine they relax,
Forgetting business problems, and the auditors and tax;
Mums just glad to be rid of work, glad it's a holiday ...
Lying on a beach towel being cooked like a raw fillet.
Bronzed young men on surf boards, trying to catch a wave,
Riding in on pounding surf, the turbulences slave.

A seductive display of bodies, parading up and down,
The young woman under the umbrella, an actress of renown.
Work weary husbands, too tired to have much fun
Eying pretty women, like ripening peaches in the sun
As young men gaze at the topless, rudely goggle eyed
One Adonis peruses the papers, his needs quite satisfied.

47

Ice creams, soft drinks, candy wrappers, odd sea shells
  Seagulls, pounding surf, the sounds of screams and yells.
The time passes quickly, as the sun smiles overhead;
Some decide to have a picnic, and a table cloth is spread
The little girl is called by her parents, it is time for them to leav
The child says goodbye to her companion,
To their world of make believe.

The soothing sound of laughter, the lapping of the waves,
The yelling of a mother, as her child it misbehaves
Bronzed young nymphets, voyeurs like bees around a hive
Fishermen and snorklers, the kids from the rocks do dive
As the finished castle lies, glistening in the sun;
An anxious mother is calling, searching for her son.

Far out in the ocean, the bathers hear faint cries
The life saver springs into action, as a bobbing head he spies
"Oh my baby, my god it's my baby!" the frantic mother scream
The father, unaware of the danger, has gone to buy ice creams
Suddenly all is silent, as the crowd scans the sea,
Parents, grab their children, as from the water they all flee.

Everyone is powerless, to stop the sea,taking its prey
As the lifesaver searches the ocean, the mother can only pray
The young man swims to the shore, sorry he can do no more,
The mother cries out in horror, her grief one can't ignore
The mother curses her inattention, to the babe left in her care,
As her husband returns with the ice creams, so unaware

To the hell of his own nightmare
Both parents not comprehending, they have bid their babe adieu
A grieving mother and father, without their babe, alone
With the angels to heaven, they pray he has flown.
Later the sun slowly sets, on waters calm and blue
Quickly the beach has emptied except for a straggler or two.
As the twilight descends the little girl returns to play in the sand

As her father jogs along the beach, she builds her wonderland
He runs into the water calling her to his side;
As he picks up a blue sun hat washed in by the tide
He playfully pops it on her head as she giggles in delight,
Together they play in the water, the sea so calm and polite.
From the sea, she hears her little friend, calling from far away

Happily, she remembers him, then her thoughts somehow stray
Not aware of the horror that occurred earlier that day
As the sea it seductively entices her, inviting her to play.
She runs into the water giggling as her dad pulls her away
While seagulls fly overhead, and fishermen haul in their nets
Father and child they leave the beach, as the sun slowly sets.

Naked babe of innocence, in floppy blue sun hat,
Sitting on a deck chair, like some ancient autocrat
Rosy cheeks, sparkling eyes, child with enchanting grin,
Covered in creams and lotions, to protect his tender skin
As the moonlight shines on the water, as it softly laps the shore
Blue hatted babe of innocence, will play on the beach no more.

Bushfire

It's so sad, it's so sad, it's so tragically sad,
So overwhelming, so devastating
No words can ever express the pain
Only two thoughts.
 Do you stay, do you go?
The fires now so very near
So wanting to save one's home
And all that one holds dear
Never really knowing, not comprehending
What agony lies in store
The raging inferno suddenly arrives,
Violently licking at the door
No escape, cut off, nowhere to go,
Just to battle on and pray
Embers leaping forward
About to create, sheer hell on earth
Mere mortals cannot cope with the Armageddon
That suddenly ascends, out of nowhere
Raging flames spreading across the land
Causing terrifying destruction absolute
Atomic explosions, the sound of hell
People huddling in cars, nowhere to go
No escape, no way out,
The decision to stay now regretted
Mobile phones used for last messages of love
People wandering, searching,
Searching, hoping without hope
Burnt out cars, twisted metal,

Bodies in the rubble, blackened nothing
Children moved to safety,
Wrong, wrong, children gone
Mothers and fathers not knowing how to cope,
How to keep on trying to survive
Loved Australians stay to fight,
Some dying together arm in arm
Neighbours helping neighbours,
Friends helping friends
Nowhere to turn, nowhere to run,
No safety anywhere
Some beloved animals saved,
Others only embers of memory
So many ashes, so many lost,
So many cut at the start of life
Families separated, desperate for news,
Fearing the worst
Joyful reunions,always hope
The relief of knowing loved ones alive
Others bereft not able to cope,
Not understanding, their lives in tatters.
The Red Cross, Volunteers
Even the Media,always there offering help
Our brave, brave, courageous firefighters
Continuing the unending fight
Men banding together to fight
To save the remaining properties left
Communities pulling together,
Trying to offer some sort of comfort

Some finding the courage to go on,
To start anew and hope once again
Hate only for the depraved monster
Who caused this horrific nightmare
Donations pouring in,
Our country sharing of its heart and also the pain
Sam the koala, a worldwide symbol of survival
Hope, love and trust
This is a time in Australian history
That will never be forgotten
To all who have lost families and homes,
No words can offer comfort
One can only cry out in silent agony
So sad, so sad, so senseless!
Let us re-address mistakes,
And dream of a better future to come.

A Tribute

To
AUSTRALIA

And
The Aussie Character

The Aussie Male

The Aussie male years ago, cripes, he had it rough!
Making something of this land
Mate,that was really quite tough
The Overlander, Shearer, Squatter and Drover
It's easy today in a four wheel land rover
But the Aussie male still has a nagging fear
Of a pub with no beer, or a woman too near

Remember to wed him, or bed him, can be tough
Yet he's a sensitive fella, beneath all the bluff
But for marriage the Aussie's a hard man to nail
Except in the outback, where they wed you by mail
They love you and leave you, they can't stand the mush
Even romancing young Sheilas they do in a rush
So down at the pub with their mates drinking stubbies

They discuss politics, women,
Their wives and their hobbies
Recession, stocks, unemployment,
Footie, racing, tennis and cricket
Pokies and gambling, any Sport they'll be in it
They flirt with the sheilas, but they now call them birds
But liberated women they run from in herds

Some take pride as real bloody knockers
But a true blue hero they always honours
They will always give the underdog a hand
Surviving in the cities, they dream of the land
Their one great virtue, they'll give their soul for you
If they think you're fair dinkum and real true blue.

Southern Cross Goddess

Southern Cross Goddess, olive, light, dark skinned or tan
She came to this country and she helped tame the land
She lived with floods, fire, drought, even hunger
She fought snakes, bushrangers, alone in the Mulga
She stood with her man in the bush,and the city
Believed in his dreams, courageous and gritty
With his seed in her womb came a new generation
She reaped and she sowed and gave birth to a Nation

They say Motherhood and virtue are their own reward
Yet with the passage of time she felt ignored
She had bred the Nation, yet she felt segregation
She stood up for her rights, and she got the vote
Victorious the Suffragettes were filled with hope
Yet back in the kitchen Mums felt no privation
The care of this Nation their one motivation
Then in time our loved ones went to War

The women wept as they stayed minding the store
Sweating in factories and farms, as he fought overseas
Yet, her man would soon have the bloody foe on his knees
Then at Gallipoli like lambs led to the slaughter
Anzacs buried the dead and their blood flowed like water
Back home women prayed their loved ones had survived
As young men half alive off the ships they arrived.
Mum, go back to the kitchen, or play nurse role instead

Your man's back home, though they filled him with lead
Then, without really knowing a new wind was blowing
Emancipation showing- Oh where were we going?
More babies and nappies while men tilled the land
No, they didn't need women to give them a hand
Then another foe to fight in another bloody War
Silently we women went back to minding the store
Then Victory ours, so many dead and women in mourning

With no more tears to shed, a new day was dawning.
A new wave of European immigrant, she came
New customs new habits, yet their needs all the same
More babies and nappies while their men tilled the land
Mini skirts, Rock N' Roll, The Bee Gees and Bandstand
Free love, Vietnam, Acid and turning on Teenies
Flower power, hippies and polka dot bikinis
Discrimination, sexual revolution along with pollution

Female lawyers, judges, mayors, a new devolution
Germaine Greer, Cosmopolitan, abortion and the pill
Lives changing, as our own needs we fulfill
Asian immigration, marriage, divorce, stress on the job
This fight for survival of dignity can rob
Change, change, orgasm, climax, even casual sex
Drugs, Aids, evolution, revolution, what's coming up next
Women head of households, not needing a mate

While others pray to God it isn't too late
The Internet, mobile phones, climate change, it's all bizarre
Yet, proud women of Australia, don't forget who you are
With our blood, sweat and tears, we helped build this Nation
Let's not see it destroyed through our own dissipation
Through these changing times, We will somehow survive!
Loving this land, filled with pride, strong, determined ALIVE

Dinkum Aussie

At 93 she looks at you, with a mischievous smile that shines
Her hair is well groomed and her eyes still twinkle
Time and the sun have lined her well loved face
But her mind is alert, and filled with wisdom and curiosity
Her laughter fills the room, a girlish giggle can often be heard
The television blazes, the sound gently muted to her ears
Questions are asked, and wise words of wisdom given
She listens to all that is said, and has such interest in life
Dinner for two is prepared with the walker close at hand
Microwaves not foreign, but regarded as a necessary thing
Food is simple, but expertly prepared with experienced hands
She lives alone, but daily is touched by so many lives
Adored by neighbours, and so loved by attentive family
Pain riddles her delicate frame, shoulders are shrugged
"That's life!" she says "one has to get on with it doesn't one!"
At times a paint brush is still used, a talent oblivious to time
Cricket and tennis, watched and cheered with patriotic pride
A good book so enjoyed, the companion constantly by her side
Pain pills are eventually discarded, as they dull the active brain
A glass of wine enjoyed, only 9% when taken from the cask
This dear sweet lady embraces each day with outstretched arms
She is indicative of this country, and an inspiration to all
She wears the years with graceful dignity
With a joy of life at 93 years of age that is extraordinary.

(In loving memory of Ann Curlewis my Dad's last love)

The Dingoes Cry

I howl at the moon and cry out in the night
Cries meant for me alone, and my pack
Letting out all intensity, afraid of nothing
This vast land was mine before you came
Fences may try to keep me out
But I exist and I will thrive despite you all
I can be your friend or your foe
Do I come in the night and take babies away?
How dare you accuse me of what I did not do
I can be a companion tamed by those who know me
I give this country part of its character
And I will roam free despite you all
Fear me or admire me, I am here, I do exist
Howling for all that I dream of all that I need
Travel with me or respect and leave me alone
Let me run wild through the outback untamed and free
Through deserts and grasslands, forests and bush
Not like you bothered by life's failures or triumphs
Knowing that another sunset always exists for me.
This land is my kingdom, come visit, run wild with me
As I watch civilization steal my land and claim ownership
Only my Aboriginal friends have an understanding of me
Oh yes, I howl at the moon, observing the Southern Cross
Along with my pack, I howl for this country's soul.
As we exist and survive in this dry, parched, sunny land calle
Australia..

A Tribute To Henry Lawson

Today I found a little book
And dusted off the grime
A book of Aussie poems
Left me by my Mum

Dear Mr Lawson
I know this is presumptuous of me
But late last night in bed
My aesthetics you did feed
Verses so brilliant
They deserve their pedigree

Poems of our cities
Of the Australian bush
Romantic verses of hope
Or cynical despair

You even spoke of Banjo
His verse you did deride
His vision of the bush
A view you did not share

As our poet laureate
Our lives you justified
Poems so very simple
So easy to comprehend

"The Shearing Shed", "Ruth","Bill",
 "The Shame of going Back",
"The Man From Snowy River"
Verses and dinkum Aussie characters
One could so easily befriend

I sat up for hours
Respecting every line
Discovery on every page
The true essence of Australia,

Thank you, Henry Lawson
Thank you Banjo Patterson
The great bards of my country
Thank you for inspiring me.

Open Windows Of The Heart

My windows are all opened wide
And the sun shines even in the rain
But if there were no windows
My world would still be beautiful to behold
Due to the one that makes me feel so alive
And in the darkness, love would always be my light
So I would paint pictures of beauty
No blank walls, but walls of imagination
Views of wild Western Australian flowers
Blue skies, forests, mountains and stark deserts.
Children laughing, playing in backyards
White sheets flapping on a Hills hoist
Families playing ball, picnicking on the beach,
Friends drinking beer gathering round a barbie
Sunny sea shores, and lovers holding hands.
Starry moonlit nights, awesome sunrises and sunsets
Unwind, take time to see the beauty within Australia.
I'm so thankful to share its wonders with my love
Living each day with a heart filled with joy
Our sanctuary in the suburbs filled with all life holds
In the open windows of my mind and heart.

The Seasons

In

AUSTRALIA

Summer

Blessed are the Seasons that come and go
Summer days of rapture on hot burning sand
Blessed is Mother Nature as passions flow
Warmed by the sun, pulsating savage land.

Autumn

Colours ever changing, red, purple, yellow, brown, green
Soft, gentle days, balmy breezes, a vibrant blessed wonderland
Bush and towns find relief from the unrelenting heat of summer
As young birds take wing flying across this alluring stunning land.

Winter

Take me in your arms and warm my heart
Protect me from the wind and biting cold
Lie with, me by the campfire and fill my soul
Desire me, do not this night your passion withhold.

Spring

Sunlight rains down on us from the blue skies above
A scent perfumes the air, breezes sway to a haunting refrain
flowers awake and burst into bloom, a profusion of colour
Winter slowly fades, as rivers flow giving life once again.

Southern Cross Sky

Love me Aussie woman
As under the Coolabah we lie
And I'll love you forever
Beneath the Southern Cross sky.

The Southern Cross Stars

Let us sleep here under the Southern stars
And feel such simple, quiet, content
No people, no bother, no fuss
Let's be young again and innocent

The night soft and caressing
The leaves our blanket on the ground
The world a place of peaceful calm
With sounds of nature all around

No time constraints or rules
Obligations or wounds agape
Unseen fears to tie us down
Only this surreal magic landscape

A place of inner solitude
The stars a cover for our bed
The breeze a tender lullaby
The moon our guardian overhead

You and I as one at last
With a gentle touch, a soft embrace
This land is where we belong
Entwined together in time and space.

Land Of Blue Gums, Wattle and Eternal Sun

One travels far and wide to many different lands
Yet the call of my country of birth keeps beckoning me back
This is my land, this is my home, the land of my birth
A gratitude that cannot really be captured in words
A feeling of pride, of belonging, of freedom and kinship
Of knowing here, there is a haven from a turmoiled world.
Blue skies, sunshine and the sound of pounding waves
Or is it just my heart answering your siren call?
You are our "Lucky Country" born of convict slaves
Rising out of darkness into the light
Shining like a beacon, calling to all, come and visit me
Stay awhile, learn all about us that you can,
I am proud to live in this golden brown welcoming land
And we who thrive here, proudly call it… Australia.

ABOUT THE POET

Brisbane –born ELIZABETH WATERHOUSE worked from the age of ten in theatre, then television for many years. After travelling overseas to continue her career as an actress, Elizabeth became much in demand as a professional model in London and New York.

Eventually, Elizabeth became President of The Woman of the Motion Picture Industry of New York and as a producer/ writer/film editor, she worked for the Will Rogers Institute Charity. On her return to Australia she worked once again in television, and also began another career as a writer/lyricist and composer.

In yet another aspect to her life, Elizabeth is now a Book Publisher and editor and will soon release her romantic Poetry Book "A Dozen Roses of Love." She has co-written with R.e. Taylor the very popular book "Aussie Yarns and Australian Legendary Folklore", and her novel "Hobo O'Riley Jr" is receiving positive reviews on her Facebook blog and will soon be released in print worldwide.

www.ingramcontent.com/pod-product-compliance
Lightning Source LLC
Chambersburg PA
CBHW060424050426
42449CB00009B/2125